THE GÜELL PALACE

The building at the start of the 20th century. It is still possible to see on the end wall the fresco *Hercules Seeking the Hesperides* by Aleix Clapés

THE GÜELL PALACE

Text
Antoni González
Raquel Lacuesta
Jaume de Puig

Photographs
Ramon Manent
Montserrat Baldomà
Francesc Morera

An outstanding building

Gaudí was commissioned by Mr Güell to undertake this quite extraordinary building as the extension to the Güell family residence in the nearby Rambla. A passageway, which still exists, was to connect the main floors of the two buildings. This is the reason why the palace was built in a district that was already undergoing a significant process of urban deterioration and not in the new extension to the city, on which building work had begun in 1860 and which would link up Barcelona and the neighbouring towns.

The rooms in this singular town residence are laid out around a central space, facing away from the street and the inner courtyard (the large gallery on the main façade is less a projecting bay window than an enlargement of this inner space and the lattice windows on the south façade offer protection from people staring in rather than from the sun). This large central space, of strikingly vertical proportions (eighty square metres in floor surface area by almost twenty in height), takes on the functions proper to the traditional Mediterranean central patio. In addition, the spatial sequences that this provides apparently exaggerates the reduced dimensions of the building (the whole site measures roughly five hundred square metres). One of the features of the palace is the large number of oblique perspectives via windows, doors and openings that Gaudí designed to connect up the different spaces that are laid out around the central core.

Along with this evocative space and the rooms on the main floor surrounding it, we should emphasise among the building's most important elements the rear façade with the shaded canopy and gallery, the floor below ground level and the roof, where twenty exposed brick or decorated chimneys keep company with the spire containing the light that illuminates the central hall on the main floor.

The fine quality of the woodwork is also worthy of attention. Types of wood have been chosen that are perfectly suited to the various uses made of them. Building conifers (white and red pine, and deal) have been used as weight-bearing elements in the joists and ceilings. Broad-leaved species (beech) are used in some of the ceilings and windows; fine hardwoods (sycamore, bulletwood, red river gum, teak or iroko, walnut and oak) in some of the decorative woodwork; and beautiful broad-leaved species (ebony, blackwood and Maracaibo boxwood) in decorative elements of the most important rooms.

As regards the general features of the palace, one of the most controversial has always been the structural system. The occasional critic, in his enthusiasm, has gone so far as to state that the palace's "rationality" means that it should be considered an "anticipation of the architecture of the decade 1920-1930". For other experts, however, the structural system of the Güell Palace may be considered confused, the conclusion being that the building should not be so positively valued as is generally the case. The two opinions, however, have no solid base.

In fact, the structure of the house was never planned overall from the very outset, but was adapted to the formal and spatial requirements of each floor. The layout of the supporting elements (walls and columns alike) does not therefore respond to the criterion of homogeneity and clarity that was considered rational by the modern movement of the twenties. It need hardly be said that this is no demerit. Gaudí employed the structural elements that interested him in the way that interested him in order to give shape to what meant most to him in architecture: space, which is the real protagonist in the Güell Palace.

Wrought-iron ornamentation representing the coat of arms of Catalonia surmounted by a helmet and an eagle

The entrance hall, coach house, stables, main staircase and mezzanine floor

The main entrance to the building is a double one, so that carriages could be manoeuvred more easily. The arches, made of stone from Garraf (from the quarries owned by Mr Güell in this massif close to Barcelona) are parabolic and closed with open-work wrought-iron gates. The two spaces immediately behind these gates form a double hall, on either side of which stand polished marble columns supporting the mezzanine floor. The ceilings of these two spaces, the highest in the hall, are decorated with tiles laid out in a concentric pattern, forming six flat vaults.

The place where the reception area stands today was once the porters' lodge, connected with the basement via the spiral staircase.

On the left-hand side of the central staircase we can still see a stone platform with four steps leading up to it, which served for mounting a horse or getting into a carriage. Once beyond the two American oak doors decorated with wrought iron, the visitor crosses a floor that, to all appearances, is made of small flagstones but is in actual fact made of wood (Scotch pine) in order to muffle the noise made by the passing carriages, and gains access to the coach house, which is an attractive space of a somewhat lower height under a flat ceiling of red ceramic tiles alternating with others of a blue floral design on a white background (from the Pujol i Baucis factory in Esplugues de Llobregat) and lit by a double window that gives on to the patio of the rear façade.

Access can be gained from the coach house via a spiral ramp down

The ground floor

to the basement, where the horses were stabled (two cast-iron rings in the shape of a unicorn, which served to tether them, may still be seen). The animals could then be taken outside

Wrought-iron balustrade

The hall on the ground floor with the main staircase
The outer gate seen from inside

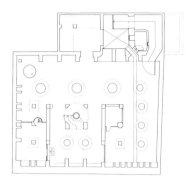

The basement

Mushroom capital in the basement

via another ramp located on the south side, which gives on to the inner patio where the rain water was also collected and where the groom's quarters stood. Two dogs' heads made of iron, with their corresponding rings, are still visible in this patio. Worthy of mention in the stables are the mushroom-shaped exposed brick capitals and columns, which are one of the best-known of all Gaudí's architectural landscapes.

Right in the centre of the hall on the ground floor is the main staircase, flanked by Garraf marble columns, which leads up to a landing where there is a large two-coloured glass screen depicting the four red bars on a gold background of the coat of arms of the territories that formed the Crown of Aragon and Catalonia.

On the landing, two doors lined with repoussé metal plaques combining Mudéjar and Renaissance motifs with plant and floral incisions give access to the mezzanine floor, which opens out on to the hallway on the ground floor via a series of barred windows. The door on the left leads to a further hall, where the grand staircase rising to the main floor begins, which is where the building truly assumes the structure of a palace.

The grand staircase, built of granite, is dimly lit at one of the corners by a polychrome stained-glass window bearing the owner's initials, EG. Above the first flight of steps, wrought-iron brackets support two beams; above this there is a balustrade-bench made of blackwood with ebony lattice work. Well worth contemplating is the ceiling, with its rich wood panelling in tropical hardwood (bulletwood) and wrought-iron embellishments. The adjoining small hall also has an interesting ceiling made of red river gum and deal.

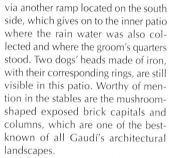

Exposed columns and capitals in the basement
The spiral ramp leading to the basement

The main floor. The main hall and chapel

The grand staircase turns to the left after the fifth step and opens out onto the main floor, where the rooms are laid out around a central space. Although these rooms have not as yet been restored, they are open to the public because of their great interest.

Four spaces follow on from the bay which the visitor first reaches. The first three, marked off by the arched gallery supported on columns which give on to the gallery on the main façade, are: the anteroom or vestibule, the "transit" room (or "lost in transit" room, as it was known to the family) and the room for visitors. The fourth space was reserved as a powder room for the ladies attending concerts or parties and has a toilet.

The anteroom has two arches with their corresponding large windows, in addition to a coffered ceiling in hard woods. The transit room corresponds to the centre of the gallery, which pro-

jects out over the street. It has five parabolic arches, which rest on four columns with hyperboloid capitals which, combined with eight shorter columns, are grouped in threes on common triangular-shaped plinths in a singular triple façade ensemble of remarkable spatial effect. The coffered ceiling above also forms a filigree of fine woods with wrought-iron floral appliqués. The upholstered armchairs with oil-painted leather (dating from the 18th century) were part of the palace's original furnishings.

The principal attraction of the visiting room, which has three further arches, is the extraordinary beauty of the ceiling, with a complex, solid reticular structure of twisted bars, one metre in length, positioned vertically and joined by diagonally-crossed twisted gilt iron struts. All these coffered ceilings are made of hard wood (mainly oak and bulletwood). The panelling in the room for receiving visitors and the powder room is also in oak.

The anteroom and room for visitors have four stained-glass windows (two

◁ Vestibule on the mezzanine and the grand staircase

Plan of the main floor and corridor linking the palace with the Güell residence on the Rambla

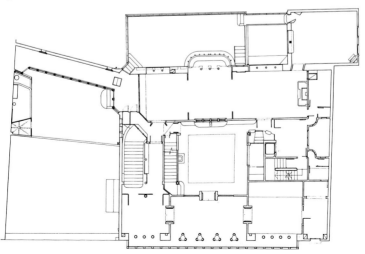

in each), placed symmetrically on either side of the upper windows of the gallery. The four are all the same shape and size and have lead-sealed plaqué and cathedral stained glass. A frieze painted in grisaille and silvered yellow frames a panel decorated with Hindu lotus leaves, in the centre of which stands a medallion. The two medallions in the anteroom depict two persons attired in the late sixteenth century manner and those in the room for visitors are King Lear and Bertram, Count of Roussillon, both of whom are characters in two of Shakespeare's plays.

The transit room leads into the spacious central hall through two large doors, which are magnificent examples of marquetry. At the far end of the hall sits the bench, consisting of a long marble seat with a back, originally of brocatelle, backing on to an alabaster block, blood-red in the style of the East, from the quarry in Garraf. The small shelf in the centre at present supports a marble bust of Antoni Gaudí by the sculptor Matamala.

On the west side stands the chapel-oratory, a small enclosure protected by a further two doors of Maracaibo boxwood (*gossypiospermun praecox*) similar to those above, decorated with plaques of tortoiseshell and horn studded with metal, which frame, both outside and inside, twelve copper panels painted in oils by Aleix Clapés. Those on the inside depict the twelve apostles. When open, the doors revealed the altar table and a small gallery with walnut wood seats from which the liturgy could be followed, thus converting the noble hall, which often staged balls and concerts, into a setting for religious devotion. The oratory was restored in 1998, at which time the brass facing for the walls was revealed and cleaned and polished.

The old organ keyboard stands on the left-hand side of the oratory, discreetly separated from the main central area by means of a column and reddish marble balustrade that reproduces the folds of a curtain.

The room is decorated with a series of murals in oils, also done by Aleix Clapés, depicting *St Isabel, Queen of Hungary, Giving Her Crown to a Poor Man; Peasant Family Praying at the Foot of a Boundary Cross*, also entitled *Have Mercy, Lord*; a portrait of the Catalan philosopher Jaume Balmes; and *Young People at Play*.

The room's main feature is the large parabolic-profile dome that crowns it. This stands on four sub-arches which are also parabolic and is lined on the inside with hexagonal plates of reddish alabaster. Natural and artificial light penetrate through tiny holes perforated in it.

On the east side of the hall there is a flight of steps, marked off by a parapet and a lattice grille in blackwood and ebony with ivory inlays (like the handrail on the organist's stool) of Arabic inspiration, which leads to the viewing gallery, the outward extension of the hall, where the musicians played on festive occasions. Presiding over the hall on the level of the first landing stands the bust of Eusebi Güell, immortalised by the sculptor Rossend Nobas, which seems to maintain a permanent dialogue with that of his architect. In fact, the bust which he had placed on the pedestal was that of his father, Joan Güell, and only posterity replaced the father's bust with that of the son in homage to the patron who had the palace first built. In addition, Joan Güell was also immortalised in the plaque decorating the pedestal, which depicts the monument dedicated to this illustrious Catalan (built in 1888 at the intersection of the Rambla de Catalunya and the Gran Via de les Corts Catalanes).

From the gallery we pass into a small private apartment which years later, when the building was occupied by the Theatre Museum, was to be the office of Àngel Guimerà (1845-1924),

Columns in the room for visitors

The parabolic dome over the central hall

the poet and dramatist from the Canary Islands who had settled in Barcelona. Access may also be gained from the gallery to the staircase that leads to the floor above, where the bedrooms were located.

◁ View of the central hall on the main floor

◁ The central hall; at the rear, the large marquetry doors which open to reveal the chapel

To the right, the chapel restored in 1998

The dining-room and the private apartment

In the third bay on the main floor, next to the rear façade, there are three spaces separated by walnut partitions where the dining-room and private apartment stood, respectively. The former has the huge fireplace designed by the architect Camil Oliveras, a friend and associate of Gaudí's on several projects, and this links from behind with the pantry and a room perpendicular to the terrace, which housed the billiards room and drawing studio for the count's daughters. The walnut furniture in the dining room is part of the palace's original furnishings and was made in the workshop of the furniture maker Francesc Vidal Jevellí. The private apartment occupied the other two spaces and served as a place for meetings, rehearsals and piano concerts.

In the third space there is a large polychrome stained-glass window which filters the light that enters from the inner courtyard of the block. Borders of lead-sealed plaqué glass painted in flat inks containing animal, plant and geometrical motifs frame three translucent glass windows; the one in the centre depicts a historical scene set in the late sixteenth or early seventeenth century, with soldiers armed with pikes, swords and muskets, against an architectural background. The whole scene is a splendid illustration of acid engraving with different inks that produce the illusion of depth.

The design of this stained-glass window is probably by Camil Oliveras, who was responsible for the decoration of the whole room, which also employs the same ornamental motifs on the friezes and wooden panelling of the skirting, ceiling and fireplace.

The lattice grill in ebony and ivory which separates the viewing gallery from the hall

Motifs which, in addition, pre-date the aesthetic of *Modernista* movement and are a direct echo of the English iconographic repertoire of the school of William Morris. There are two further stained-glass windows of similar characteristics in the former billiards room attached to the dining-room.

The most interesting feature of the central private room is the large gallery, separated from the inner enclosure by four parabolic arches on columns, which projects towards the

Detail of the walnut dining-room fireplace designed by the architect Camil Oliveras

The upper part of the dome; in the background, one of the windows in *trencadís*-style stained glass.

rear façade. It is closed off by means of folding shutters. These adapt to the convex shape of the gallery, forming two sections with a base that retreats as it rises; the lower section is occupied on the inside by a bench that adapts to the oval contour of the gallery, whose back is covered in Cordovan leather decorated with floral motifs, a faithful reproduction of the original, which was replaced in the 1992 restoration. Above the seat is a series of twelve windows finished in a pointed arch and separated by ebony columns. When the shutters are closed, light can enter through four rows of small rectangular holes covered with old glass of different colours.

The visual sequence of the three spaces corresponding to the central part of the three bays — transit room-main hall-private apartment — is achieved via arches and windows that provide a leisured view of the coffered ceilings.

The latter, like the friezes that adorn the walls, are done carved walnut.

In a wing immediately next to the private apartment stands the glass-lined passage which links up with another open patio and connected the palace with the Güells' former residence, at number 37 on the Rambla (this entrance no longer exists). In this passage, Eusebi Güell's children had a small museum with ceramic fragments, altarpieces, iron, clothing, furniture and other items. A large glass screen converts this area into a kind of cloister-patio, which creates an atmosphere of both uniform and diffuse brightness. The screen fills the spaces between the columns with an alveolar-shaped iron design crowned with a triangular-shaped one in imitation of a pointed arch. The stained-glass set in the iron framework is of a cathedral type, hand painted, with a rough texture and pale colours.

Gallery of the private room on the main floor

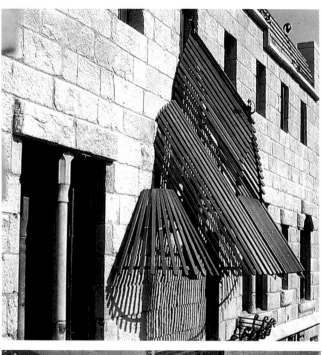

The rear façade. The terrace

From the right-hand side of the passage, access can be gained to the terrace at the rear of the palace, which overlooks the inner courtyard of the whole block. From here one can contemplate the whole architectural and decorative richness of the rear façade, whose epicentre is the gallery. This emerges from the middle of the main floor and is crowned with a balcony of Catalan wrought iron, which projects from the second floor and is covered, in turn, by a slender canopy made of wooden slats of African scented mahogany in the *brise-soleil* manner, jutting out obliquely over the middle of the patio.

The lower part of the gallery corresponding to the level of the bench inside is covered with turquoise and cobalt tiles laid like a chessboard.

The middle body, which stands out farthest, contains the twelve windows mentioned above, whose upper part takes on a garret-like form. The roofs of these garrets are built with glazed tiles of a rusted yellow colour (the original tiles came from the Pujol i Baucis factory and the new ones, put in place in 1992, are a reproduction made by the SOT Ceramic Workshop), which form an undulating outline with crests and ridges, in the upper part, and tiny gargoyles in the lower part, through which rain water can drain away. The intrados of the arches is also covered with blue tiles like those of the base.

Some Gaudí experts see in these shapes zoomorphic or fantastic elements, such as a giant serpent or, perhaps, a sea monster, where the crests and ridges of the arches are the breastplates for defence and protection, whereas the lower gargoyles are the animal's feet. They may be no more than beautiful shapes.

The upper body of the gallery is subdivided, in turn, into two parts, the lower one crowned with tiles of the same colour as those mentioned before, shaped flat and raised at one end in such a way that when mounted over the following tile they create a ridge that makes the whole structure watertight and gives it a continuous look.

The terrace area is closed off by a reticulated lattice partition to make it more private. The present one was installed in 1991 and is made of sapeli from Guinea.

A gangway built over the inner courtyard of the stables provides access from the terrace to the former billiards room, which opens on to the terrace through a large metal door similar to that in the dining-room, where the visitor can see the only wrought-iron column in the whole house, on which remains of the original painted surface are still visible.

The canopy on the rear façade

Detail of the inner courtyard terrace with its lattice partition

The back staircase. The flat roof

The only way to the flat roof is by the back staircase, which is reached through the vestibule behind the old organ console space next to the altar in the main hall. The back staircase is made of iron with stone steps and beechwood handrails, with an ingenious placement of the hanging iron bars, which provide the uprights for the handrails and which, fitted together, are suspended from a beam situated on the penultimate flight of the staircase. On the first-floor level, a magnificent folding grille door worked in wrought iron separates the service area from that of the apartments.

◁ The weather vane and lightning conductor which crowns the lantern on the rooftop

Four shell-shaped lunettes flank the lantern

Plan of the roof indicating the location of the 20 chimneys

The roof in its overall conception is not a strange one (several years were still to pass before *Modernisme* introduced unusual roofs in Barcelona, many of them with no great justification in terms of construction or climate, and Gaudí designed the strangest one of all, that of the Casa Milà). The roof of the Güell Palace is simply flat, like so many others in Barcelona: flat tiled surfaces, proper to a Mediterranean climate, with a profusion of tiny constructions - stairwells, pigeon lofts, ventilator shafts, chimneys - which emerge from a sea of washing hung out to dry. The flat roof of the Güell Palace is, nonetheless, a fantastic one.

Fantastic (in other words, created by the imagination), because Gaudí in his imagination recreated in it the microcosm of a traditional flat roof. The shapes, which are in turn the

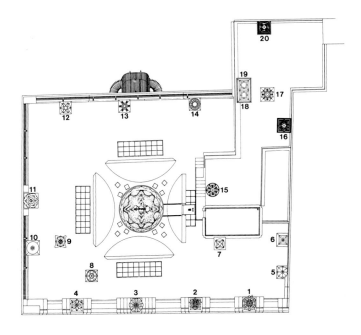

recreation of timeless forms, emerge from a flat tile base alongside stairwells and handrails which could hardly be more ordinary. The classic dome assumes a peculiar conical form flanked by four shell-shaped lunettes and crowned by a weather vane-lightning conductor made of iron, brass and copper, while the traditional chimneys have been transformed into twenty beautiful decorated or exposed brick sculptures.

In the fourteen decorated chimneys, the three elements (base, shaft and cowl) come in a great wealth of shapes: bases shaped like pyramids with square, mixed prismatic-conic or cylindrical-conic bottoms; four-sided cylindrical or prismatic shafts; cowls in shape of cones or pyramids (with rhombuses and triangles, segments of a sphere, intersected cones, or spiralling convex fluting).

The materials decorating the surfaces are also varied: *trencadís* — fragmented tiles — (chimneys 1, 5, 6, 7, 8, 10, 12 and 14), marble (13), glass (2, 3 and 4), glazed earthenware (9) or fragments of vitrified sandstone from the inside lining of old lime kilns, like those covering both chimney number 11 and the spire-light.

The ceramic *trencadís* come from Catalan enamelled tiles, some of which were manufactured as early as the late eighteenth and early nineteenth centuries (such as the white ones decorated with blue geometrical or floral motifs, or the green ones mottled in white) and others manufactured by the Pujol i Baucis factory from at least 1870 onwards and by the La Esperanza factory in Onda (Castellón). The earthenware *trencadís* comes mostly from the Pickman factory in the Cartuja of Seville and, in lesser quantity, from the factories of Mariano Pola

The south face of chimney number 9

y Cía in Gijón, San Juan in Seville, Sargadelos, Santander and even from factories in England (J. & G. Meakin of Hanley), Germany (Villeroy & Boch of Mettlach) and France (Lunéville, Clermont Fils, W.G. & Co. of Limoges) from the mid and late nineteenth century. The few pieces from the Royal China in Vigo and the Vargas factory in Segovia were put in place during restoration work undertaken in the 1970s, as were some fragments of glazed tiles placed on other chimneys, which are unmistakable due to their characteristics and colours.

Tiles of the same period or manufacturer, similar to the originals, which were still to be found on the market or were reproduced by craftsmen, were used in the restoration of these chimneys carried out in 1992. The earthenware *trencadís* chimney (number 9) was restored with pieces of old plates from the very same Pickman factory, following the original composition. On the south face, however, there is one small gesture of a contemporary nature in a reference to Barcelona's status as the Olympic capital when the restoration work was being carried out: the Cobi mascot and emblem of Olympic Barcelona in memory of the 1992 Games.

The chimneys lined above the main façade and the first one that stands out on the eastern façade still have the original decoration on the bases

Detail of the rooftop, with chimneys 9, 10, 11, 12 and 13 (in the foreground)

Another detail of the rooftop, with chimneys 8, 9 and 11

and shafts; that of the cowls, however, has been lost. During the 1992 restoration, these were covered once again with traditional materials, the new design being entrusted to four Catalan artists. The cowl of number 1 was undertaken by the ceramist J. Gardy Artigas in his workshop in Gallifa; those of numbers 2 and 4 were designed by the painters Robert Llimós and Joan Mora, respectively; that of number 10 by the painter Gustavo Carbó Berthold; and that of number 3 was the joint work of all four and of the architects responsible for the restoration of the building.

Chimneys number 5, 6, 7 and 8 still have the original ceramic decoration on the cowls, shafts and rims of the bases. The central facings on the bases were covered with tiles in the 1972 (number 8) and 1992 restorations, in this case designed by architects: number 5 by Pau Carbó; number 6 by Antoni González; and number 7 by Domingo García-Pozuelo.

◁ Chimney number 11, covered with fragments of vitrified limestone

Chimneys 5 (to the right) and 6

27

The main façade

Once outside in the street, the visitor can contemplate the main façade by way of a summary and farewell. Its main characteristic is, perhaps, its stern appearance, accentuated by the gallery on the main floor, supported by consoles of balanced profile, which runs the whole length of the façade, rising at the ends to the floor above.

This gallery and the lower floors follow a vertical rectangular rhythmic thrust that softens the sternness of the whole and which, in turn, is interrupted by the two catenary arches that mark the threshold and gates and provide the façade with its maximum expression, without sculptural ornamentation except for the isolated lilies at the first-floor level.

The most important decorative element is the lattice-grille on the spandrel between the two arches, a masterpiece in wrought iron, where the smooth strips and metallic mesh-work combine to form the shield of Catalonia, conceived as a semi-column entangled at the base with the foliage of the hibiscus in the small window with spiral bars and, at the top, a helmet crowned by an eagle with outstretched wings. On either side, studded metal strips anticipate in their undulations the *Modernista*-style whip lash effect.

Equally remarkable are the two entrance gates, also made of iron, which were the first of their kind to be used in Barcelona. Here wrought iron can be seen in all its plastic variations: door panels with smooth and twisted bars, mesh work thickened with the very same bars to block visibility from the outside and simple mesh-work of

Windows in the main façade

greater transparency; stone edgings coiled around with corner-post serpents and crenellations, fastened with studs, and parabolic tympanum decorated with wrought iron coiled sinuously in a whip-like movement which surrounds the motif emblematic of the owner of the residence owner.

At the heart of these tympana, the initials E and G appear as a fresh tribute in Gaudí's constant homage to the industrialist and patron who had the audacity to believe in him and made his work not only possible but celebrated worldwide.

Partial view of the main façade

Areas that cannot be visited for the time being

The restoration work being carried out in the palace means that visits have to be restricted to the areas described thus far. There are, however, other rooms of great spatial and ornamental richness.

On the mezzanine floor, to the right of the large stained-glass window which presides over the access staircase, are the rooms reserved initially for Mr Güell's office, administration and archives and, at a lower level, perpendicular to the rear façade, the old private library, which has a larch wood lattice-grille.

To the left of the large stained-glass window, in one corner of the vestibule, there is a small room with a fireplace opening on to the Carrer Nou, whose walls are lined with marble slabs from Garraf with gilt floral inlays. This small room was probably used as the office of Mr Güell's secretary or private administrator, the poet Picó i Campomar, or else was used as an antechamber.

Climbing the back staircase brings us to the area originally reserved for the pantry, kitchen and other minor rooms. The pantry is on the same level as the main floor and the remainder are between the floors, on the same level as the viewing-gallery above the main hall.

A narrow staircase begins at one side of this gallery which leads to the second floor of the building, where the family's private apartments were situated. The latter were laid out around the gallery with windows that were closed with beech, glass and brass lattice work, overlooking the main hall. It would appear that the musicians or choirs installed themselves in this gallery on the occasion of a soirée or choral concert; thus the music could be heard perfectly, bearing in mind the special architectural and acoustic conditions of the hall.

The first of the rooms, used as a place for private conversations, has a remarkable, beautiful fireplace designed by Camil Oliveras and decorated with a white marble panel designed by Alexandre de Riquer, depicting St Isabel of Hungary. This panel, signed in 1883, must have come from one of the residences of Eusebi Güell and his wife, Isabel López.

In the north bay stood a bedroom with dressing-room and two further bedrooms. All these private rooms repeat the theory of arches and columns in the rooms on the main floor. The coffered ceilings are made of beech and teak (or iroko), and in some cases have a brass plating. The study still has its beechwood ceiling and walls, a small marble fireplace with parabolic arch and the stained-glass windows with their acid engraving. The bedroom furthest to the west has a polychrome stained-glass window depicting the figures of Hamlet and Macbeth and the Swedish coat of arms.

The inner bedrooms maintain this same array of arches and columns, with the exception that in the married couple's bedroom, these elements are decorated with fanciful wrought-iron plant shapes of *Modernista* inspiration in which "Salve", the linked initials E and I corresponding to the names Eusebi and Isabel, and the date 1895, can be made out. The parabolic fireplace designed by Gaudí also stands in these rooms.

In the west wing stood the bathroom and toilets (decorated with tiles from the Pujol i Baucis factory, which still remain today), and another room of considerable dimensions with a white marble fireplace along classical lines.

In general, the doors and windows on this floor are worked with oak and sycamore veneer (*acer pseudoplatanus L.*).

Former office and administration area on the mezzanine

Climbing further up the back staircase, we reach the attic — where in former times there were eleven bedrooms for the servants, the kitchen and laundry — which opens on to the upper part of the dome via large parabolic iron windows, with leaded polychrome stained-glass windows with cathedral glass fragmented in the manner of *trencadís* tiles.

Access can also be gained via the back staircase to the area occupied, in a somewhat contrived way, by the organ, which was practically destroyed during the Civil War. In 1992, the organ was removed and replaced by a new one, enabling this small space to be redistributed, with emphasis now

Plan of the second floor, where the family's private rooms were

given to the two parabolic polychrome stained-glass windows which had been condemned to stand in a corner practically hidden from view.

The restoration of the Güell Palace

The palace was used as the Güell family residence until it was confiscated during the Civil War. Several years later, in 1945, it was purchased by the Diputació de Barcelona (Provincial Council) which, from 1954 onwards, used it to house various sections of the Theatre Institute. The main aims of the restoration and refurbishing work undertaken since 1982 are to make it easier for the general public to visit the building and to turn it into a "museum of itself", in addition to permitting other suitable representative and cultural functions to be held here.

One further aim is to solve the normal problems arising from the age of the building materials as well as the transformations and wear and tear due to use. Also, in some cases, to solve certain questions pending since the outset, as the creative process of the Güell palace naturally did not escape the traditional controversies raised by the basic antinomy of architecture: the tension between plastic and construction elements.

What matters, in the final analysis, is to give the building back its authentic character, exactly as Gaudí himself understood it: "not in the restricted sense of replacing elements of a particular style or period, but in the sense of restoring things to their proper place and function", and for this reason — also in his own words — "practising architecture without archaeologisms; instead of copying forms, producing ones that are full of their own spirit."

Two approaches to the project have been used at the same time in recovering the authentic character of the Güell palace. On the one hand, painstaking work is being undertaken to identify and recover all the building or decorative elements. Doors, windows, shutters, lattices, awnings, metallic mechanisms and ornaments, stained-glass windows, stone steps and paving; all the elements, in a word, that have been lost or damaged are being replaced with complete faithfulness to their original shape, material, texture and colour.

On the other hand, however, in certain specific instances, the work has been affected by the other concept of an analogous non-mimetic restoration that necessarily involves prior critical analysis of the object inherited and a permanent dialogue with it in the design of formal solutions. A dialogue that has been present particularly as regards involvement with the roof, one of the most attractive areas of the palace, yet where the hand of Gaudí —for reasons which we are unaware of— revealed itself at its most contradictory.

The Güell Palace

Location: Carrer Nou de la Rambla, 5. Barcelona. Catalonia. Spain.
Designed by: Antoni Gaudí i Cornet, architect (1852-1926).
Commissioned by: Eusebi Güell i Bacigalupi, industrialist (1846-1918).
Date of construction: 1886-1890.
Present owners: Diputació de Barcelona.
Present use: Building representative of the institution that owns it, open to the public.
Restoration: Begun in 1982, financed by the Diputació de Barcelona, with support from the Spanish Ministry of Culture and the European Community (EC).
Directors: Antoni González and Pau Carbó, architects, with the collaboration of Raquel Lacuesta.
Construction company: Urcotex. Barcelona.
The Güell Palace was declared a national monument in 1969 and is one of the three works by Gaudí to have been singled out as a World Heritage Site by UNESCO in 1985.

Details of the gargoyles and the slatted screen of the gallery on the rear façade

Detail of the rooftop, with the gangway that leads to the lantern

Eusebi Güell i Bacigalupi (1846-1918)

Son of Joan Güell i Ferrer (1800-1872), doctrinaire champion of the economic protectionism of the early part of the century, Eusebi Güell was a man with a solid economic, juridical, scientific and humanist background, an enterprising businessman and a politician faithful to the ideals of conservative Catalan nationalism. In addition, he was a patron of the arts and letters in Catalonia, a patronage which materialised, above all, in the figure of the architect Antoni Gaudí.

In 1871, Güell married Isabel López i Bru, the daughter of the first Marqués de Comillas, Antonio López y López, by whom he had eight children. The Güell-López's first residence was the Fonollar palace, located in Carrer Portaferrissa, numbers 7-9, in Barcelona, which linked up with the Comillas Palace through the gardens at the back of the buildings.

It would appear that the friendship between Güell and Gaudí began in the carpentry workshop of Eudald Puntí, which was making a glass display case designed by the architect and commissioned by the Comella glove shop. During the International Exhibition in Paris in 1878, Güell saw this glove display case and, back in Barcelona, contacted Gaudí. This was to be the beginning of a close association and a particularly fruitful patronage, which was to lead to several works that are renowned worldwide: the remodelling of the estate owned by the family in Les Corts, the couple's new residence in Carrer Nou de la Rambla, the church in the model industrial village for manufacturing textiles that Güell had founded in 1891 and the private housing estate which in time was to become the Güell Park.

In 1918, just before he died, Eusebi Güell was raised to the peerage as Count de Güell by King Alfonso XIII.

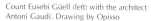

Count Eusebi Güell (left) with the architect Antoni Gaudí. Drawing by Opisso

Antoni Gaudí i Cornet (1852-1926)

Antoni Gaudí was born in Reus (Baix Camp, Tarragona), the son of a family of coppersmiths, a fact that he was to associate with his special concept of space. He came to Barcelona in 1870 and studied architecture there. Before qualifying in 1878, he worked as a draughtsman for the master builder Josep Fontseré (with whom he worked on the monumental fountain in Ciutadella Park in Barcelona) and with the architects Leandre Serrallach and Francisco del Villar Lozano (on the niche room in the basilica of the monastery of Montserrat). He also undertook various other projects in association with the architect Joan Martorell i Montells (who later recommended him for the task of continuing the church of the Sagrada Família).

Put briefly, two stages can be distinguished in Gaudí's work. The first is characterised by a desire to break with the academic tradition and medievalist eclecticism prevailing in European architecture by striking out on a new personal path of formal and spatial expressiveness, based largely on Hispanic-Moslem art, yet free from revivals of historical authenticity. In chronological terms, this period predates the appearance of the European movements that ran parallel to *Modernisme*, Gaudí's early work in fact representing one of its foundations. The main undertakings of these first fifteen years in his profession are: the Casa Vicens (1883-1885), in Barcelona, El Capricho (1883-1885), in Comillas (Cantabria), the Güell estate (1884-1887), the Güell Palace (1886-1890) and the Col·legi de les Teresianes (1889-1890), all three in Barcelona, as well as the Episcopal Palace in Astorga (1887-1893). It was in the Güell Palace that the architect went further and developed the experiments made in his early work, both in spatial

aspects and decoration, which he conceived in a personal manner and where he made a good number of contributions that were to constitute the basis of his later repertoire.

Gaudí's mature period coincided with the appearance in Catalonia of *Modernisme* and in other countries of parallel movements (Jugendstil, Art Nouveau, Liberty, etc.). As regards the architect's output, this represented the final break with all references to historical styles and the achievement of a plastic art and personal structural forms, in other words, what was later to become known as the Gaudí aesthetic. Dating from this period are: the church in the Colònia Güell (1898-1914), the Nativity façade to the church of the Sagrada Família (1893-1926), the Torre Bellesguard (1900-1902), Güell Park (1900-1914), which was the first garden city experiment in the whole of Spain, the Casa Batlló (1904-1906), the Casa Milà (La Pedrera, 1906-1910), the restoration of Majorca Cathedral (1904-1914) and the schools of the Sagrada Família (1909), the last work begun by the architect.

From 1918 onwards, Gaudí concentrated on building the Sagrada Família, where he had a small lodge that served as a studio, where he lived until June 10 1926, when he died, at the age of 76, as a result of the injuries sustained after he had been run over by a tram two days before.

In the palace, as in all of Gaudí's works, his extraordinary architecture stands out for the richness of his concept of space and the originality of the decoration, which do not always require large budgets, as has been stated. It may be true that in the Güell Palace there were no limits to the budget available, and this is evident in the type of materials employed. Yet in

The coach-house on the ground floor at a time when it was still used for the family's carriages

other works — such as the Col·legi de les Teresianes, undertaken immediately following the palace, or the schools of the Sagrada Família — it is, if anything, the lack of resources that was to make Gaudí's architecture even more imaginative.

Gaudí's imagination is based, moreover, on taking maximum advantage of the static and aesthetic properties of materials and traditional construction methods, without involving himself, in this sense, in what is understood today as modern architecture, which is founded in part on new materials. Gaudí was unquestionably more an innovator than simply a forerunner.

The main hall, shown as it was furnished in about the year 1890

Buildings by Antoni Gaudí i Cornet
Locations and visiting times

Palau Güell

Carrer Nou de la Rambla, 5. Barcelona
Bus: 14, 18, 38, 59
Metro: Line 3 (Liceu)
Tel. 93 317 51 98
Visiting times: 10.00 a.m. to 2.00 p.m.
and 4.00 p.m. to 8.00 p.m.
Closed on Sundays and public holidays
To arrange specialist visits:
Tel. 93 402 21 73

Casa Vicens

Carrer Carolines, 18-24. Barcelona
Bus: 16, 17, 22, 24, 28
Metro: Line 3 (Fontana)
Generalitat local railway network
(Gràcia)
Private home
Only the exterior can be seen

Col·legi de les Teresianes

Carrer Ganduxer, 85-105. Barcelona
Tel. 93 212 33 54
Bus: 14, 16
Generalitat local railway network
(Tres Torres)
Visiting times: Saturdays from 10.00
a.m. to 1.00 p.m.
Guided tours can be arranged by
telephone

Casa Bellesguard

Carrer Bellesguard, 16-20. Barcelona
Tel. 93 417 54 01
Bus: 14, 22, 58, 64
Generalitat local railway network
(Av. del Tibidabo)
Visits to the gardens and exterior of the
building during the day

Casa Batlló

Passeig de Gràcia, 75. Barcelona
Tel. 93 216 01 12 (IBERIA de Seguros)
Bus: 7, 22, 24, 58
Metro: Line 3 (Passeig de Gràcia)
Visiting times: from 8.00 a.m. to 3.00 p.m.
Free entry to the hall and reception area
of the IBERIA de Seguros company

Casa Milà (la Pedrera)

Passeig de Gràcia, 92 / Carrer Proven-
ça, 261-265. Barcelona
Tel. 93 484 59 79 (Fundació Caixa de
Catalunya)
Bus: 22, 24
Metro: Line 3 and Line 5 (Diagonal)
Visiting times: daily from 10.00 a.m. to
8.00 p.m.
Permission to film or take photographs
must be requested in writing to the
director of the Fundació Caixa de
Catalunya.

Sagrada Família

C. Marina, 253. Plaça Gaudí. Barcelona
Tel. 93 455 02 47 (Sra. Teresa Martínez)
Bus: 19, 34, 43, 50, 51, 54
Metro: Line 5 (Sagrada Família)
Daily visiting times: October to June
from 9.00 a.m. to 7.00 p.m.; July to
October from 9.00 a.m. to 8.00 p.m.;
August from 9.00 a.m. to 9.00 p.m.

Finca Güell: pavilions and fence

Avinguda de Pedralbes, 7 / Avinguda
Joan XXIII. Barcelona
Tel. 93 204 52 50 (Càtedra Gaudí)
Bus: 7, 22, 64
Metro: Line 3 (Palau)
Visiting times: Weekdays from 8.00
a.m. to 2.00 p.m.

Finca Miralles: gate and boundary wall
Passeig de Manuel Girona, 53. Barcelona
Bus: 6, 16, 70, 74
Metro: Line 3 (Maria Cristina)
Visits at any time

Casa Calvet
Carrer Casp, 48. Barcelona
Tel. 93 318 43 25
Bus: 7, 18, 19, 22, 35, 39, 41, 42, 45,
47, 55, 56, 58
Metro: Line 1 and Line 4 (Urquinaona)
Visits to the hall only

Güell Park
Carrer Olot, s/n. Barcelona
Bus: 24, 25
Opening hours: September from 10.00
a.m. to 8.00 p.m.; October from 10.00
a.m. to 7.00 p.m.; November to
February from 10.00 a.m. to 6.00 p.m.;
March from 10.00 a.m. to 7.00 p.m.
April from 10.00 a.m. to 8.00 p.m.; May
to August from 10.00 a.m. to 9.00 p.m.

Casa-Museu Gaudí (inside Güell Park)
Tel. 93 214 64 46
Visiting times: daily from 10.00 a.m. to
2.00 p.m. and from 4.00 p.m. to 7.00
p.m. Closed from December to February.

The Crypt at Colònia Güell
Santa Coloma de Cervelló (Baix Llobregat, Barcelona)
On the road from Sant Boi de
Llobregat to Sant Vicenç dels Horts
Tel. 93 661 29 36 and 93 630 24 01
(for tourist and school visits); and 93
402 21 73 (specialist visits arranged by
the Architectural Heritage Service of
the Diputació de Barcelona)
Visiting times: Weekdays from 10.00
a.m. to 1.30 p.m. and from 4.00 p.m.
to 6.30 p.m.; weekends and holidays
from 10.00 a.m. to 1.30 p.m.

The Episcopal Palace at Astorga
Plaza de Eduardo de Castro, s/n. León
Tel. 987 68 82 (Los Caminos Museum)
Opening hours: in summer from 10.00
a.m. to 2.00 p.m. and from 4.00 p.m. to
8.00 p.m.; in winter from 11.00 a.m. to
2.00 p.m. and from 3.30 p.m. to 6.30 p.m.
Guided tours available.

Casa Fernández y Andrés (Casa de los Botines)
Plaza de San Marcelo. León
Currently owned by IBERCAJA
The offices may be visited during
working hours.

El Capricho
Sobrellano Park. Comillas (Cantabria)
Tel. 942 72 02 70 (El Capricho cafe-
teria and restaurant)
Visits: it is advisable to book by tele-
phone

© Diputació de Barcelona
Third edition: May 1999
English version by: Duual, S.L.
Graphic Design: Francis Closas
Layout: Jordi Paré
Diagrams: Elisabeth Valls
Published by: Institut d'Edicions
Typesetting: Teknocrom, S.A.
Printed by: CEGE
Dipòsit legal: B-21714-1999

The photos on pages 20 (below),
22, 24, 27 and 32 are by Montserrat Baldomà;
the photo on page 15 (below) is by Francesc Morera;
and the remaining photos are by Ramon Manent.

Cover: detail of the ironwork of the main gate.
Inside front cover: the building as it was at the beginning of the 20th century.
The fresco *Hercules Seeking the Hesperides* by Aleix Clapés can still be seen on the end wall.
Inside back cover: stained-glass window on the grand staircase.
Back cover: the lantern on the rooftop. The gallery on the rear façade: detail of the ceramic roof.
Detail of the main gate of the palace.